The Simplicity of Making Money

The Simplicity of Making Money

Editor & Designer

Sherman A. Jones

Cbookspublishing and Bookstore
Cbookspublishing.com

The Simplicity of Making Money

Cbookspublishing and bookstore

619 Copeland Dr.

Cedar Hill, Texas 75104

www.cbookspublishing.com

ISBN: 978-0-9849733-7-8 *(Soft-copy)*

The Simplicity of Making Money

Published by Cbookspublishing

A Division of Cbookspublishing and Bookstore
619 Copeland Dr. Cedar Hill, Texas 75104

An American Publishing Company

The Simplicity of Making Money

TABLE OF CONTENTS

Preface

From this book, *The Simplicity of Making Money,* a financial freed gives a permanent release loosing the shackles of money poverty. In this book, there will be an uncovering **"accent"** the negatives; thereby, the "overcomer" will begin **"accentuating"** positive, profitable money to a lasting outcome." This book endeavors to be childlike, fun, easy to read and understandable. "Why did you seek Me? Did you not know that I must be about My Father's business?" But, they did not understand the statement which He spoke to them" (NKJV Luke 2:49-50). "The oversight of Israel on the west side of the Jordan for all [is] the business of the LORD and is in the service of the king" (NKJV 1 Ch 26:30). This is the religious foundation that serves as a foundation for making money.

It has been said more time than can be counted, "A fool and the fool's money shall part?" Well! This is the accenting of the negative. The other is: "Money does not grow on trees?" However, the tree is a source of money, and trees are the paper that allows the printed form of money call a "Bill." **"MONEY TREE!"** Turning a tree into money is an **accentuation** of the positive. From a fools' understanding, it would appear that there would be no difference between the words "Accent and accentuation" since they, both have the same prefixes.

This prelude or pre-introducing will be with us leaning back to the proposed wording—**accent and accentuation"**—for clarity (clear).

9

The word **"accent"** is just **"pronouncing or saying something."** There is no need to belabor this unnecessarily with any great length. (e. g., The person that is homeless; for most, all know there is no reason to rob this old chap because there are no moneys in his pockets because no money has been earned or made; **this too is simplicity**). The **"accentuation of"** is the looking at circumstances and doing something about one's circumstances. It is the importance of a developmentally designed, theory, and research put into practice that shows the result (i.e., **"Moneys in our pockets"**).

Here is a problem. Going back and forth to jail is to the giving away any money made. This is called **"nullification,"** the act of canceling something out. The, repeatedly, going back and forth to jail over time will turn a person into a "mad dog;" the scripture says, "As a dog returns to his own vomit, so a fool repeats his folly" (NKJV Proverb 26:11).

Going forth into this book, this book will serve as a **"Help Guide"** to the making money. The methods of this book, *The Simplicity of Making Money,"* are easy and simple in the profession of "money making." *[The sport of making money has its own defined vocabulary, and the money makers will gain the skills of* **"talking-the-money-talk."** *This book, The Simplicity of Making Money, will provide the vocabulary for the money talking one will need for business transactions. At the beginning of each chapter,* **"Key Money Words"** *will be there to attract moneys into the pockets of the money makers. This statement, in the introduction will become much clearer in the introducing of this book's layout and inclusion.]*

This prologue will not thrash a "dead horse to death" just to compose some thick book to look dressy delivering nothing. When it comes to making money, most do not want "to-know" any more than what is necessary to get the money, right? Just show the money! The principles in all money making are to stay on top of the "game" of making money. It is time to begin! This little book, *The Simplicity of Making Money* will provide the need skill to get the "money maker" started, going forward, using the money making blueprint, and support to get into the game. Let's Go and Get it!

Formula

1. _____ $1+1=\$2$
2. _____ $2+2=\$4$
3. _____ $4+4=\$8$
4. _____ $8=8=\$16$
5. _____ $16+16=\$32$
6. _____ $32+32=\$64$
7. _____ $64+64=\$128$
8. _____ $128+128=\$256$
9. _____ $256+256=\$512$
10. _____ $512+512=\$1,024$
11. _____ $1,024+1,024=\$2,048$
12. _____ $2,048+2,048=\$4,096$
13. _____ $4,096+4,096=\$8,192$
14. _____ $8,196+8,196=\$16,392$
15. _____ $16,392+16,392=\$3,2784$
16. _____ $32,784+32,784=\$6,5568$
17. _____ $65,568+65,568=\$131,136$
18. _____ $131,136+131,136=\$262,272$
19. _____ $262,272+262,272=\$524,544$
20. _____ $524,544+524,544=\$1,049,088$

Introductory "Money Words" Vocabulary

Word Master and Understanding: The building of an all

time vocabulary for, *The Simplicity Money Making* process.

Shackle(1999-2013) states from the permission of Jakes website the following:

> The 1920s and 1930s were particularly rich in American slang terms for money, some of which are still in use today. Some terms referred to money's use in purchasing food: **bacon** (as in [bringing] home), **bread, dough**, and so on. (One term for counterfeit money was **sourdough**.) Other terms referred to the green color of [the] American bills: **cabbage, lettuce, kale, folding green, long green** (para. 18).

Buy v.

1. to acquire the **possession** of, or the right to, by paying or promising to pay an equivalent, especially in money; purchase.
2. to acquire by exchange or concession: to buy favor with flattery.
3. to hire or obtain the services of: The Yankees bought a new center fielder.
4. to bribe: Most public officials cannot be bought.
5. to be the monetary or purchasing equivalent of: Ten dollars buys less than it used to.

Sell v.

1. to transfer (goods) to or render (services) for another in exchange for money; dispose of to a purchaser for a price: He sold the car to me for $1000.
2. to deal in; keep or offer for **sale**: He sells insurance. This store sells my favorite brand.
3. to make a **sale** or offer for **sale** to: He'll sell me the car for $1000.

4. to persuade or induce (someone) to buy something: The salesman sold me on a more expensive **model** than I wanted.
5. to persuade or induce someone to buy (something): The clerk really sold the shoes to me by flattery.

squander

1. to spend or use (money, time, etc.) extravagantly or wastefully (often followed by away).
2. to scatter. noun
3. extravagant or wasteful expenditure.

frugal

1. Economical in use or expenditure; prudently saving or sparing; not wasteful: What your office needs is a frugal manager who can save you money without resorting to painful cutbacks. Synonyms: thrifty, chary, provident, careful, prudent, penny-wise, scrimping; miserly, Scotch, penny-pinching. Antonyms: wasteful, extravagant, spendthrift, prodigal, profligate.
2. Entailing little expense; requiring few resources; meager; scanty: a frugal meal. Synonyms: scant, slim, sparing, skimpy. Antonyms: luxurious, lavish, profuse.

Introduction

The adventure begins over into this book, *The Simplicity of Making Money*, as an analogy, the plane is out on the a runway of making moneys with the purpose of flying into the sky of **"Unlimited Money."** Believe it! Once getting started with the wings of money making desire stretched, the trip is fast with every now and then a few turbulences. However, the excitement is worth sacrifices and out weighs the worst of times. Taxiing up the runway the next dollar constantly gaining monetary speed for that ultimate thrust before a full throttle beginning (the experimental). The cruise from one dollar to the next shoots the money maker upward into the sky of money; where, money makes itself. It has been said, pertaining to making money, that "the sky is the limit." This too is an illusion. This means in the living of a life, making as much money as one can make, there will be left a million times more for the next person to get. Actually, there is no end to money. Be not dismayed about what the next person has gotten or will get. Just make money. There are no territories or boundaries as to the making of money. Making moneys is global. Stop being Dumb!

HEADS-UP. . . " Stay focus," a money tip, in this book, can come "*at anytime, under any heading, or on any page without warning.*" This is about the **$$CASH$$** and is not about enjoyment for the sake of enjoying of a book. This is **Making Money Easy & Simple** in Accordance With the Laws of the Land.
Heads-up. . .

Scarcity, as to resources, only applies to the present ownership of economic wealth and money in the bank. There is still the sky of money, the stars of money, the planets of money, and the world upon the top of the worlds of money. If money was only in "rock and roll," then, there would be a scarcity of resources. But outside of the box, a group of young black artist saw the "sky of money" and came up with "rap." **They reached for the sky of money.** The business industry is using their "raps" voice-overs songs on their products like never before from/to their advertising schemes. They are using **"got your jingles."** Say it with me, **"Beam me up Scotty?"** LOL!!! A great sense of humor and a positive engagement of is not being denied " the money." Being money minded is an awesome "Key" and will be discussed in the chapters to follow: **Enthusiasm & Persistence.**

Studying Jesus, one must accept the conclusion that Jesus is the world's greatest businessperson—from carpenter to heading the world's largest organization, "the Church." Jesus's business was his father's business, which was his job on earth. Jesus knew how to built because this what carpenters do. Jesus had a business, job and a ministry. Jesus said, "A certain nobleman went into a far country to receive for himself a kingdom and [then] to return. So he called ten of his servants, delivered to them ten minas ([ancient money]), and said to them, 'Do business till I come'"(NKJV Lk 19:12-13).

Going forward into making money, *The Simplicity of Making Money*, will ruffle a few feathers, especially in the religious "church house" community. The root cause of life's poverty in several communities is the fault and failure of certain organized churches (not all). "Dumb preachers, with a dumb message as a pretense calling it "God's message to the church." As a word of caution, this only applies to minority few preachers!   You know: **"The Holy-er Than Thou Crowd"** holding on to their supposedly <u>"corner market of heaven with no golden streets, the world is about to come to an end (end timers), and sell you have preachers."</u> The scripture says, "And they saw the God of Israel. And there was under His feet as it were a paved work of sapphire stone, and it was like the very heavens in its clarity" (NKJV Ex 24:10).

Beware!   Beware!   Beware!

"Beware of dogs, beware of evil workers, beware of the mutilation!"
(NKJV Php 3:2).

There is a crowd that will will say that making money is an evil. These same people, if one would inspect their lives, will have two and three bank accounts.   This is hypocrisy at its worst!   Those are the real liars that teaches nothing and will say anything because they don't know any better, and the truth is not in them.   Any preacher, that preaches about "Sin" every Sunday is a fool and do not know God nor what God is all about.   Yes, this author said it!   Jesus and scripture is this author's support for such who says, "Why did you seek Me?   Did you not know that I must be about My Father's business?" But they did not understand the statement which He spoke to them" (NKJV Lk 2:49-50).   Preacher man, all know "Sin," but where is the "Money Making Lesson" that will help one out of "SIN!"   The teaching of making money the right way can stop some sinning and give to God a bigger "tithe and love offerings."   Believe it!   **"It is almost a sin to be broke."**

If it is not a sin to be broke, being broke can and will make one commit a sin, sooner or later!.   Listen to what Jesus said:

All who ever came before Me are thieves and robbers, but the sheep did not hear them. I am the door. If anyone enters by Me, he will be saved, and will go in and out and find pasture (pasture is green and to a sheep a **golden paradise**). The thief does not come except to steal, and to kill, and to destroy (**dumb preacher**). I have come that they may have life, and that they may have it more abundantly (NKJV Jn 10:8-10).

The only person in the church house that has a new car, a fine house, and money in the bank is the preacher; there is something wrong with that picture, "Agreed?" The preacher gets up Sunday after Sunday talking about "nothing;" other than, "how sinful everyone and everything is, who shot John," and about a church that is built upon a "Rock." The Devil just loves that kind of preaching. The devil is in the church house even before the preacher because he is the "prince of the power of the air" (NKJV Eph 2:2). Satan is a great listener! All communication goes through the air. This is why it is so easy for Satan to defeat so many, **"TALKING OUT LOUD TELLS THE DEVIL AND OTHERS EVERYTHING."** From the old school, it is said that the only conversation that is not heard is that conversation that is *"WHISPERED IN THE EAR OF ANOTHER."* **IS THE MESSAGE RINGING LOUD AND CLEAR?**

It is easy for the Devil to steal the children of these parents that are going to that sad, sick churches of **"Dumb Preachers."** All the Devil needs to do is pose a question to these misguided that listen to dumb preaching. Jesus was a listener but did not now follow any dumb preacher. Satan is the great master twister of God's word. Did not the Bible say, "And I will make thee like the top of a rock: thou shalt be a

18

place to spread nets upon; thou shalt be built no more: for I the LORD have spoken it" (KJV Eze 26:14)?

This introduction is not only introducing what all is going to learn over in this book, but this introduction is also going to give spiritual strength and a foundation to handle what is over in this book. This is an **unorthodox introduction.** **"Orthodoxy"** has never been general tenets of the masses as to all of making money.. "Therefore whoever hears these sayings of Mine, and does them, I will liken him to a wise man who built his house on the rock [strong foundation]: and the rain descended, the floods came, and the winds blew and beat on that house; and it did not fall, for it was founded on the rock [strong foundation]" (NKJV Mt 7:24-25).

The Simplicity of Making Money raises one above temptation. Just as Jesus was tempted in the wilderness will be attempts tempting the maker of money by the Devil, "And when the tempter came to him, he said, If thou be the Son of God, command that these stones be made bread" (KJV Mt 4:3). "Did not the preacher say that the church is built on a 'Rock,' and the church is God's business?'" Answer: Yes! The Devil will twist the understanding of the stated and will shout, telling us "Let's 'Rock and Roll'" (dope pusher and crack heads). This is what got so many of our young people in prison today. The Simplicity of Making Money is not about "selling" some rock or "selling" other junks that are illegal. However, The Simplicity of Making Money is freedom to perpetual profit.

There are more legal products that one can sell than there are illegal products, and the pay rate the end is greater as to the legal products. Many of our young people in our communities are selling illegal products from listening to Dumb Preaching that does not share with them alternatives in business. Let's say it again, Dumb Preaching coming from Dumb Preachers. Bear in mind God accepts all preachers, "the sent" and "the went." However, all preachers have not accepted God and the direction of his word in the directing of his people into health and wealth. Jesus said to those "Dumb Preachers" this in his word:

> Many will say to me in that day, Lord, Lord, have we not prophesied in thy name? And in thy name have cast out devils? And in thy name done many wonderful works? And then will I profess unto them, I never knew you: depart from me, ye that work iniquity (KJV Mt 7:22-23).

I warned us up front that this book, *The Simplicity of Making Money*, will ruffle a few feathers and at the same time be entertaining. There is nothing complicated or evil about making money. For those that have known me down through the years, I have always had a "Ministry" (Presently, president of Fathers Evangelical Ministry); I have always had a business (Presently, president of Cbookspublishing and Bookstore; the company that is publishing this book that you are reading: accessed at www.cbookspublishing.com), and I have always had a job (writing books for a living). I have always made money. Making money is like "shooting marble" or playing a "video game on a computer. It is "FUN!"

Here is what most people fail to realize, and the "Dumb Preacher" do not want you to know, in his church (not God's Church) that as a function all are doing business activities daily and at the same time have a job. Balancing a checkbook is business. Paying bills is business. Choosing what to buy and when to buy it is business. This is what creates the problem. Most church goers have never been told that running a household is a type of business. This is because if these households (doing great jobs running households) would accept the great business of their operations and extended to other business they too would have more wealth. With this understanding, the Devil will not be able to talk these household out of their monies without giving them something in exchange. Therefore, running a home is a business, but what is it that these households not doing? "Building UP and UPON their present business" of making more money from *The Simplicity [principle] of Making Money.*

Now with eyes open, receive this repeat thought in our being: **"Making Money is Simple!"** The simplicity means easy but getting the money means doing. Working, *The Simplicity of Making Money*, is no robbery. Even, Jesus admitted that he had to work his business, his ministry, and at the same time help others. To this Jesus said, "I must work the works of him that sent me, while it is day: the night cometh, no man can work" (KJV Jn 9:4). There is no excuse not to work and not to making money the right way, if, one's parent is going to the wrong church with a "Dumb Preaching

21

Preacher" does not mean that anyone has to be dumb. The preacher cannot stop the making of money, and it is the personal responsibility of the individual to study to know the truth. "Study to shew thyself approved unto God, a workman that needeth not to be ashamed, rightly dividing the word of truth" (KJV2 Ti 2:15). For observation follow the instruction of a wise preacher who said:

> Go to the ant, thou sluggard; consider her ways, and be wise: Which having no guide, overseer, or ruler, Provideth her meat in the summer, and gathereth her food in the harvest. How long wilt thou sleep, O sluggard? when wilt thou arise out of thy sleep? Yet a little sleep, a little slumber, a little folding of the hands to sleep: So shall thy poverty come as one that travelleth, and thy want as an armed man (KJV Proverb 6:6-11).

In God, all life is a business and is spiritual because God is a spiritual being. *The Simplicity of Making Money* is not an evil ordeal. Don't let someone planted a bad seed in your life that has your pockets empty. Decide right now that to make yourself some money. This will be be covered over in the rest of the book. Change the negative person's thinking, get from around all persons that are negative because that person is in your way and will be a stumbleblock. Here is what a wise Preacher (Solomon) said:

Hear, O my son, and receive my sayings; and the years of thy life shall be many. I have taught thee in the way of wisdom; I have led thee in right paths. When thou goest, thy steps shall not be straitened; [but] when thou runnest, thou shalt not stumble. Take fast hold of instruction; let her not go: keep her; for she is thy life. Enter not into the path of the wicked (dumb preachers), and go not in the way of evil men (devils and criminals). Avoid it, pass not by it, turn from it, and pass away. For they sleep not, except they have done mischief; and their sleep is taken away, unless they cause some to fall (KJV Pr 4:10-16).

How about a little more "clip art" warding off any boredom?

But, how can one get bored making money? Even the prostitute will admit, although, the money she make has a lot of "hard work" in it—making the money is not boring. Get the point?

In this book, *The Simplicity of Making Money*, we are going to get to see money from every horizon, plane, & above.

Along with "enthusiasm and persistence," there is a widening of the visionary imagination in the fertile field of money making awaiting a harvest. In this book, the chapters to follow will show that the bible is not opposed to *The Simplicity of Making Money*; but rather, the Bible encourages earning a living (employees) and make money (obedient servants of the given talents)

Here is a great Biblical example:

Jesus saith unto them, My meat is to do the will of him that sent me, and to finish his work. Say not ye, There are yet four months, and then cometh harvest? Behold, I say unto you, Lift up your eyes, and look on the fields; for they are white already to harvest. 36 And he that reapeth receiveth wages, and gathereth fruit unto life eternal: that both he that soweth and he that reapeth may rejoice together. And herein is that saying true, One soweth, and another reapeth. I sent you to reap that whereon ye bestowed no labor: other men labored, and ye are entered into their labors. (KJV Jn 4:34-38).

The world would not all the great, beautiful cathedral as wonders if some was not doubling the talents from, *The Simplicity of Making Money.*

Here is another Clip Art for amusement:

Looking at this clip art, try not to miss the great point of making money. *The Simplicity of Making Money* is not just prescribed for only men. Women have, down through the years, been some of the greatest money makers. Why? Money knows no color, gender, or race. It is inedible that one will become stronger and stronger the very start of making money.

The greatest start for a book of this nature is **"Don't Procrastinate!"** As to the few definitions in this book, these definitions are an embellishment create communicating and give understanding to *The Simplicity of Making Money.* What is the money making simplistic definition for the word procrastination. **Procrastination,** for all intent and purposes, is the postponing and not getting up off your tail going forward to make money.

Here to speak, the meaning of the perpetuation is to **Create Your Own Definition of Success**, and this will follow in chapter 2. As

24

stated, it does not take a rocket scientist to make money. However, *The Simplicity of Making Money* is a sane proposition. Making money has to be done (if successfully executed) with the whole person. *The Simplicity of Making Money*, is not a bunch of "crack pushing fools" on a corner claiming this is what is meant about being simple. One of the intent of this book is to show these "crack headed selling fools" that "they have the right macho, but selling the wrong a bad product."

On the front cover of this book, *The Simplicity of Making Money*, there is a **"formula chart."** Believe it or not, this is the formula chart of every and all money making businesses, adventures, and investments (even, the fortune 500 businesses). This formula is called Jones' "Money Double Model." the "Money Double Model" will be discussed throughout this book and the chart can appear anywhere without notice. Now from spiritual speaking to the spiritual doing, here is another clip arts, this will keep us the "Energized Bunny! " "[S]eeing we also are compassed about with so great a cloud of witnesses, let us lay aside every weight, and the sin which does so easily beset us, and let us run with patience the race that is set before us," (KJV Heb 12:1),

Set Goals for Yourself & Give Yourself Time is another as to a chapter: Remember, "Rome was not built in a day!" "But let patience have its perfect work, that you may be perfect and complete, lacking nothing" (NKJV Jas 1:4).

Do not be dismayed by the usage of the Bible in the making of money. Because the scripture also goes to say, "[H]e shall have power over the treasures of gold and of silver" (KJV Dan 11:43)—and God says, "The silver is mine, and the gold is mine" (KJV Hag 2:8); therefore, "Be not slothful to go, and to enter to possess the land" (KJV Judges 18:9).

Make Mistakes, but Don't Give Up, Keep demanding! The turning of the page into this chapter is the positive belief in ourselves with the knowledge that money is never stagnant. In the place of wrong timing of missed opportunity, This is called "mistake/mistakes." It needs to be understood and realized that a mistake is not the end of the race.

The Simplicity of Making Money is the enjoining the prospects of *Making Mistakes, but Don't Give Up, but Keep Demanding.* Then comes a summary that will neatly packages everything that have been learned that have taken some a lifetime to learn.

Reference

Shackle, E. (1999-2013). *Moolah, marigolds... and a macaroni!?!*
    Retrieved from Slang Euphemisms for 'Money': http://www.fun-with-words.com/money_words.html

Money Tip

Advertise for someone and get "Paid!"
  ➤ Put the advertisement on your car and just ride around.
  ➤ Put the advertisement on your person and walk around.
  ➤ Put the advertising on your social network pages and talk.

Get Paid: Making Money is Simple.

This book, *The Simplicity of Making Money,* will get you started, and money will flow into your bank account with no stopping.

Sell the Ideas, and Get Paid.

Chapter One

Stop the Procrastination

"Money Words" Vocabulary

ATM   n. Automatic Teller Machine aka Hole in the wall

Cashflow   n. cash earnings minus cash outflows for fixed-and and working-captial investment.

Currency   n. money that is used by a country such as the United States

Debit   n. a sum deducted from a bank account

I will— but I need a little more money in my cash reserve!
I must pay off a few of these bills, first!
I will get started after the kids get a little older!

Money is never made by procrastination. "Dream-On"— create the world greatest profitable organization ever in your head. No money will ever get to the hands or to any bank until the first step is taken: **"MAKING IT HAPPEN."** The "Dream-On" is not the procrastination.

The procrastination is the "Dream-On" and no action. Many can "talk" a good game, but can they "Play?"

This is not saying dreaming is a bad thing, and this is not saying that the one dreaming did not intent to do the thing; however, "Intends are 'Broken Promises!'"

What is being said is this: The "Nursing Homes" are full of people of the procrastinated saying right now: "**If I'hada**," "**I Woulda**," or "**I Shoulda**." Remember this: "Time" waits for no one.

"Oh, how time flies!" This is the sad reality of procrastination, "time" slipped away and someone else got paid. After time has slipped away, many are right now looking back at all the missed opportunities, with now a question: "Where did the time go? Time went and left when there was no action, and the dollar was not doubled to the making of two dollars.

BE WISE. . . Study this formula chart (see fig. 1) This is the progression formula that gets rid of procrastination.

Fig. 1

$$Formula$$	
1.	1+1=$2
2.	2+2=$4
3.	4+4=$8
4.	8+8= $16
5.	16+16=$32
6.	32+32=$64
7.	64+64=$128
8.	128+128=$256
9.	256+256=$512
10.	512+512= $1024

> **Procrastinate!**   **Procrastinated!**
>
> > **Procrastinating**   **Procrastination**
>
> *Some making money act that should be in present time action, but has been given an assignment for some imaginary future time, which might or might not ever come with a loss of earnings.*

What stopped us? **Procrastination!**

At the double of 20 times your dollars starting with $1, the formula chart would have given us **$1,049,088. This is a million with a "m" dollars.** (see fig. 2).

Fig. 2

20.	524,544+524,544=$1,049,088

OVER $1 MILLION DOLLARS

Money Tip: $$$FAST CASH$$$

Sell everything that you have in your house or is in your possession that you do not want.

Cash is "sitting and looking" waiting on you; and—all you have to do is "SELL IT!"

STOP the PROCRASTINATION"

(JUST DO IT!)

Burka & Yuen (2008) gives us the " procrastinator's code" that stops and prevent the **"ACTION"** making money as follows:

PROCRASTINATOR'S CODE
(Are you one these people?)

1) I must be perfect;

2) Everything I do should go easily and without effort;

3) It's safer to do nothing than to take a risk and fail;

4) I should have no limitations;

5) If it's not done right, it's not worth doing at all;

6) I must avoid being challenged;

7) If I succeed, someone will get hurt;

8) If I do well this time, I must always do well;

9) Following someone else's rules means that I'm giving in and I'm not in control;

10) I can't afford to let go of anything or anyone;

11) If I show my real self, people won't like me; and

12) There is a right answer, and I'll wait until I find it (p. 16).

These stated 12s are the stoppers that prevent the **"Making of Money."** Remember this, no one said stopping anyone from **"earning a living."** Earning a living is nothing. All one has to do is just do what someone else says do, and they will give the residue of their Making Money. For most folk, this is all they ever get out of life: what someone tells them that they can have. This is called **"Modern Day Slavery"** Bear in mind, all slaves are not equal. One work in the house and the other works in the field.

Money makes money! **Procrastinators will never "Make-A-Dollar!"** They fear losing the one dollar. One dollar buys! This only lost is if one does not go forth and sell. The goal is doubling our investment. Do not be the novice thinker! A double of a dollar is the repetitious accomplishing a goal. It might take five or six purchases and sales—or even more, depending on the amount of the investment to see the dollar doubled, but it will never be doubled if one does not sell it.

Krause & Freund (2013) in their book, *How to Beat Procrastination: The Role of Goal Focus,* give us a a dynamic model showing us the relationship between procrastination and goal focusing during the action phase of "doubling dollars," *The Simplicity of Making Money* (see, fig. 3):

Fig. 3

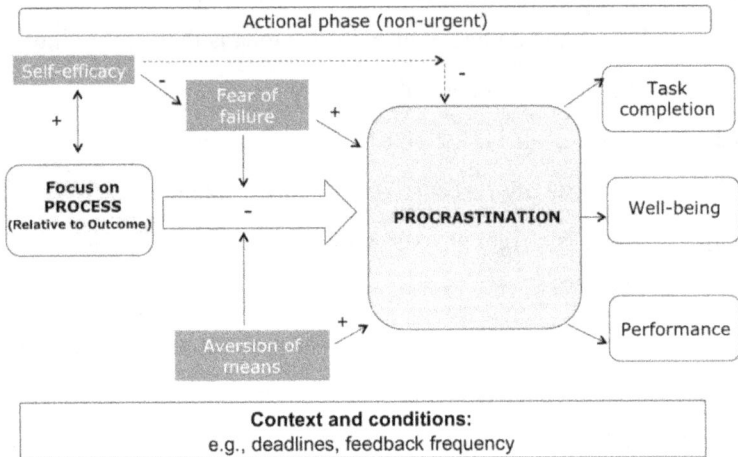

The Simplicity of Making Money depends on task completions, well-being, and performances. **Procrastination** must be done away with that usually creates a **"fear-of-failure"** and **"aversion-of-means."**

Fear of failure stops one from getting started by not opening one's hand—clenched fist stops the entrance of a dollar.

"Aversion-of-Means" is the act of turning oneself (gazing at other as they do their money making thing) away. These two negatives (fear of failure and aversions of means) are the driving forces in procrastination that would not allow one to exercise in *The Simplicity of Making Money*.

1 Dollar + 1 Dollar = 2 Dollars. . .

The Simplicity of Making Money

Reference

Burka, J. B., & Yuen, L. M. (2008). *Procrastination : Why You Do It, What to Do About It Now*. Cambridge, MA: Da Capo/Life Long.

Krause, K., & Freund, A. M. (2013). How to Beat Procrastination: The Role of Goal Focus. *European Psychologist*, doi:10.1027/1016-9040/a000153

A Bit of Money Humor

A man working for a brick making factory that never got caught like everyone else stealing bricks. Everyday he roled a "Wheel Barrel" out of the gate after the guard searched the man and the wheel barrel looking for stolen bricks. Finally, the man retired. The guard asked the man this question on his last leaving the job: "I know that all of your kind are thieves, why is it that I never caught you stealing bricks?" The retired man answered, "I was stealing "Wheel Barrels!" The scripture says, "But when thou doest alms, let not thy left hand know what thy right hand doeth: That thine alms may be in secret: and thy Father which seeth in secret himself shall reward thee openly" (KJV Mt 6:3-4).

Chapter Two

Befriend Your Competitors

"Money Words" Vocabulary

Acceptance: v. the act of agreeing to accept an offer.

Amass: to <u>accumulate</u> an item such as money, property, or goods. A company may stock up on a commodity now for future sale when it believes that a sharp increase in the price of the commodity will take place at a later date.

Aptitude: intellectual ability of an individual to learn material sufficiently so that he can properly perform the business task required on the job. Some individuals have a natural talent and tendency for specific business areas. An example is a trial lawyer with an intellectual and a quick mind for question asking and logic.

Asset: anything owned by a person or organization having monetary value, usually its cost or <u>fair market value</u>. An asset may be a specific property, such as title to <u>real estate</u> or other tangible property, or enforceable claims against others.

Average cost: total of all costs for all units bought (or produced), divided by the number of units acquired (or produced).

Budget: the total sum of money set aside or needed for a purpose.

Bread-and-Butter: basic source of income; supplying the basic needs of life.

Earnings: <u>money earned</u>; wages; profits.

Moneymaking: capable of making or promising to make money: the money making part of the deal.

Percentage: <u>gain;</u> benefit; profit; advantage shared by more than one on any given money making deal.

Productive: producing or tending to produce goods and services having exchange value.

Profitable: <u>beneficial</u> or useful.

Profit Margin: the ratio <u>gross</u> profits divided by net sales

Solvent: capable of meeting financial obligations.

Viable: <u>practicable;</u> workable:

Money Tip

In most states, an individual are allowed to buy 10 cars and resale them, every year, without having to get a dealers licence.

It's not Rocket Science. Buy IT! Sell It!

In *The simplicity of Making Money*, befriending your competitors is simply saying collaborating with competitors. Stattler (2013) wrote an article called, *The Value of Collaborating with Competitors* and stated: "You can build a friendship and exchange ideas without giving away sensitive information"(p. 5).

There are those four main purposes behind befriending:

- **Specific/targeted:** to find education, employment, stop re-offending, help integrate into the community, develop a career
- **Change behaviour:** to improve relationships, reduce unwanted behaviours etc
- **Expand opportunities:** to develop personal skills, build confidence, improve attainment etc
- **Supportive:** to build trust and resilience, reduce isolation etc (Mentoring and Befriending Foundation, 2011 - 2012).

Befriending competitors—in *The Simplicity of Making Money* concept—is not the minute to minute concerning about how much money we make v. others. However, this is a respect for others in the business of making money. It does not matter who gets to the top first. The only thing that matters is that everyone can apply *The Simplicity of Making Money* principle get to the top. One should love to say to a competitor, "We'll meet at the top!" In *The Simplicity of Making Money* process competing is never the stopping the other guys from doing all that he/she can, but it is a process of doing all that one can with no fear of other/others.

Competition is a good thing. This is stretching in the exercise of making money. Competing wards-off laziness. Competing creates drive. In (2011) Bartes stated:

> Competitive Intelligence plays one of the most important roles in the preparation of company management' decisions when creating new conditions to guarantee the company's future success in the keenly competitive business environment, and it is considered one of the most powerful weapons of the future in the hands of company management (p. 668).

It is a mad rush to the bank, daily!

Competition is good, good, and good! In the business game of making money, *The Simplicity of Making Money* has never been about self; it is about the dollar making another dollar. The selling of self and the dollar buy what is for sale. It is here the buying something with the purpose of selling that something to make two dollars: **Doubling the Dollar**. Take the two dollars buy something with the purpose of making four dollars. Take the four dollars, buy something, double the four to make eight dollars.

Get the Idea!

The only weapon one needs is the getting up off of one's behind:
Buy and Sell!

The Products are Everywhere!

I am going to get personal now: You think you do not have an idea, you may be correct! The reason that you are correct is because we have not looked **up!**

On Every Corner There are Business Signs

(Look-UP)

Look up! And again I say, look up!

Let us repeat the message: there is a sky of the money that is over and above all money that have been made; but, the sky not the limit of the money. This may sound idiotic and crazy, but it is a fact. I wish not to go to fall afield nor too in-depth and heavy as pertain to what I'm trying to get us to see. For example: there are satellites in the heavens that are producing monies that was not imagined 100 years ago. Everywhere in the heavens today there is a production money coming down. And let me be the first to let us understand, no limit has been reached yet; we only believe we can touch the sky. Even if we did touch the "sky" to all that money, where would we have the room to put all that money? However, and for now, with our feet on the ground, our one dollar, and looking up is to the everyday business advertising signs giving us ideas about what is possible. All business has either of both a sale and service components that produces the profit.

Lookup! And again, I say. . .!

References

Bartes, F. (2011). ACTION PLAN - BASIS OF COMPETITIVE
  INTELLIGENCE ACTIVITIES. *Economics & Management*,
  *16*664-669.

Stattler, E. (2013). The Value of Collaborating with Competitors.
  Managing People At Work, (370), 5.

Chapter Three

Create Your Own Definition of Success.

"Money Words" Vocabulary

As is: commercial term denoting agreement that buyer shall accept delivery of goods in the condition in which they are found on inspection prior to purchase, even if they are damaged or defective.

Alter ego: the other self. Under the doctrine of *alter ego*, the law will disregard the limited personal liability one enjoys when acting in a corporate capacity and will regard the act as his or her personal responsibility.

Amount: sum, represented by a number; frequently number of dollars.

Applied overhead: amount of overhead expenses that are charged in a cost accounting system for a production job or a department.

Bottom line: <u>net income</u> after taxes.

Business plan: a comprehensive analysis of all aspects of a business enterprise relevant to its viability, including its history, management, competitive position, market, activities, products, <u>policies</u>, finances, and projected finances.

Self-employed: individuals who work for themselves and are not employed by another. The owner-operator of a <u>sole proprietorship</u> or a partner in a <u>partnership</u> is considered *self-employed*. Those who are self-employed assume all the risks and responsibilities of a business enterprise and are subject to <u>self-employment tax</u> , in addition to <u>income tax</u> , to <u>net income</u> from self-<u>employment</u> activities. The self employment tax is paid in lieu of the Social Security <u>payments</u>.

Clayton (2011), a black young lady, Vice President of Learning, Training and Development, The Boeing Company was asked: What lessons did you learn along the way? She answered:

Run your own race. Take time to get to know who you are and what you value. Make sure the decisions you make are guided by your passions and identity. Create your own definition of success. People invent false ideas of what success looks like. If you want the corner office, go for it. If you want something else, you have to define it or you will never be satisfied (p. 6 [T+D]).

1+1=2; 2+2=4; 4+4=8; 8+8=16; and 16+16=32

I respect what "mama and daddy" told me, but it is my time, and I must live out my life in my success and not the successes of "mama and daddy." I will endeavor to hold on to the good values that was placed in me by my parents. These good values I will not compromise, but I do want to just earn a living; **"I Want to Make Money."**

Therefore, I must define my success and go for it.   This is simply saying, seeing the prize and not being denied. I will be in **"Controller of my Financial Destiny."** It is here, now, that I am working on my definition of success.

Money Tip:

Auction—Auction—Auction

Ebay and others. . . Establish a sales price and **sell** the items at the price or at an acceptable **bid price**. You can get more money for collectible Items by selling them on the internet than you can by selling them from a garage sale.

Define Your Own Definition of Success

Now you Know; Making Money is Really Simple—just sell what you have and sell that of others for a commission, since, you are making money and not earning a living. It is the open-mindedness that *The Simplicity of Making Money* is all about.

Bring Home the Bacon, Baby!

Reference

Clayton, N. (2011). Stay True to You: The definition of career success is up to you. *T+D, 65*(10), **8**.

Chapter Four

Set Goals for Yourself & Give Yourself Time

Money Tip:

Pricy Items

This is for the **Trend Setters**.   Sell you price an item such as clothe and sport equipment to such stores as Play It Again Sports, and Plato's Closet.   Nearly every retail store will sell your pricy item for a commission.   Get commissions on all **antiques**.

Additional Tip: You can buy pricy item from autions and sell for a greater value.   Stessed: Stressed: Do your home work. . . Home work!!!

The Simplicity of Making Money

Here are 10 other great business goals, given to us by Susan (2010), to help grow your business:

1. **Organize your office** – It's always nice to start off the year fresh with a clean desk. Enter all those business cards into your database or at least put them nicely away and hire someone else to enter them in.

2. **Set up a customer relationship management system** - Whether it's a manual whiteboard or a web-based tool, getting a grip on your sales funnel will help you better follow up on leads, stay in touch and provide better customer service.

3. **Make business planning part of your daily or weekly routine** – Schedule in time for writing, reviewing and adjusting your goals. Write out manageable sub-goals and break them down into actionable task lists.

4. **Delegate more** – Write out the list of tasks you can delegate and try to find someone to do them. Remember you should be working on your business not in it.

5. **Make marketing your business more consistent** – Determine the most effective marketing strategies and add them to your routine business tasks.

6. **Add social media to your marketing plan** – It's finally time to jump on the bus! Read up or talk with someone about the best way to add in social media. Proper planning at the start will help you save time and create an integrated content strategy that is more effective.

7. **Clean up your website** –Now's the time to make all the edits, optimize your pages, add to that blog, set up an affiliate program and put all the latest social media widgets to your site.
8. **Streamline your business** –Take a critical look at the services or products you are offering and eliminate those that are draining your resources and not adding to the bottom line. This may not be overnight.
9. **Automate and build systems** – Look at what tasks you do on a daily, weekly and monthly basis. Try to turn these into regular procedures that can either be streamlined, automated or delegated. Research new tools to make your work more efficient..
10. **Learn something new** –Learning something adds new skills to your palette and helps keep the passion going (Susan, 2010).

"This one thing I do, forgetting those things which are behind, and reaching forth unto those things which are before" (KJV Php 3:13).

Reach forward into the harvest after determining the goal applying one's ability. This is what Jesus had to say about this harvest as one look at one's goal, ""The harvest truly is plenteous, but the labourers are few" (KJV Mt 9:37). Who went on to say:

> I say unto you, Lift up your eyes, and look on the fields; for they are white already to harvest. And he that reapeth receiveth wages, and gathereth fruit unto life eternal: that both he that soweth and he that reapeth may rejoice together. And herein is that saying true, One soweth, and another reapeth. I sent you to reap that whereon ye bestowed no labour: other men laboured, and ye are entered into their labours (KJV Jn 4:35-38).

There is an old saying that says, "Rome was not built in a Night"? However, Rome would have never been built without a start action; afterward, much money was made. Why? Because by now, all have figured out that it is simple. Just buy and sell! However and after doubling dollars, after the sum of $1024, the work of doubling dollars becomes a more intense work requiring greater and more specific goal setting. This means that we are going to have to do a little soul searching, a little organizing, and allow ourselves time to proceed to the next step in the doubling process.

The setting of a goal for ourself is the answering the question of how to take $1024 adding $1024 for an ending profit of $2048. The goal would be, after deciding on the product, how many to buy; we have to figure out how many we have to sell in a month, how many in a week, how many in a day, and at what price. The $2048 profit will only come after all expenses; therefore, this means that we might have to make $3, 000 to get a $2048 profit. All along the way moving up the ladder of *The Simple Making Money* process, we are going to have to put it on "Paper." The failure that the average person make in the money making process is never putting "It On Paper!" We have to know the bottom line: how much we had to spend and now much is left. The Profits and the Losses! The paper is to show and remind one of where the process began and where is the progress in doubling process that simplifies the next action to be put into the process for another upward mobility for a profit margin.

The Simplicity of Making Money is the knowing from whence we started; where we are; and these will guide us as to where we are going and where we will be. These words of Jesus are our guide shared with us and states:

> He also that had received two talents came and said, Lord, thou deliveredst unto me two talents: behold, I have gained two other talents beside them. His lord said unto him, Well done, good and faithful servant; thou hast been faithful over a few things, I will make thee ruler over many things: enter thou into the joy of thy lord (KJV Mt 25:22-23).

Get Money Smart (n.d) gives us 10 reasons for setting goal associated with making money that I feel is very important:

1. You can see the possibilities you never saw before!
2. You will maintain inspiration and motivation.

3. You can see hope for better things.
4. You are able to concentrate your energy towards your desired result.
5. You have a clear vision for your future.
6. You are no longer confused about what action to take.
7. You are able to prioritize your time.
8. You can conquer procrastination.
9. Your self-confidence increases with each step taken towards your goal. (Get Money Smarts, n.d.)
10. You are focused on what YOU want to achieve.

Reference

Get Money Smarts. (n.d.). *Why Set Goals.* Retrieved from Get Money Smarts: http://www.getmoneysmarts.org/dream-smart/why-set-goals

Susan. (2010, January 9). *Top 10 Small Business Goals for the New Year.* Retrieved from New Earth Marketing :

http://www.newearthmarketing.com/blogs/top-10-small-business-goals-new-year

---

Money Tip:

All Thing Recyclable

There is in every major city 5 to 10 different metal buying facilities that pays **top dollars** for metals. (i. e., Tin, Iron, Cast, Alumunium, Copper, and Steel). Some of these medal sales for as much as $3 a pound. This mean for every 100 pounds you walk away in **one day $300.00**.

The Simplicity of Making Money.

Not just metal: **Paper, Glass, and plastics.**

Summary

Strapping Together the Pieces

In essence, we can say that this is a conclusion or a summary of the book, *The Simplicity of Making Money*. Just as we are *"Strapping Together the Pieces,"* this could be called a great book of "Money Making" clarity. As we all know, there is a competition of the spirit as to the resources that is a part of making money. God wants us to make money for the kingdom, and Satan wants us to make money to cause confusion and division in an attempt to make himself God by putting many persons in prisons.

It is in this respect that we have shown that anyone can make money without breaking the law. The resources are everywhere. Therefore, if one is not making money, one is working on earning a living a repetitive non ending process for the most part.

The Simplicity of Making Money is about the getting started with what we have, and with the determination that we are in the business of making money and not earning a living.

We can take one dollar and double that dollar turning it into two dollars. This is *The Simplicity of Making Money*. It is unlikely that an individual will invest one dollar only into the purchase of an item that one is going to sell over and over again until that one dollar become two dollars. Doubling, doubling, doubling is the simplistic money making process that anyone can use to make money.

First, you cannot be a procrastinator. This speaks volume of itself which needs no extraneous elaboration. Procrastination is just an uploaded of waiting for some future tomorrow that might never come.

Secondly, do not be afraid at of competitors. Bear in mind that we do not know everything. In some instances, our competitor can be a our information source as to a missing piece and/or gives us a lead that could be very profitable.

Then, there is the defining of your own success. This is going forth in determining the amount of hours, and the number of days that one will dedicate to the crafts of making money.

And finally, it is with goal setting that one can measure where the success has been achieved. Out of such is the giving one's sufficient time to accomplish each measurable retained earning relating to *The Simplicity of Making Money*.

After making the first money, that first money will make the rest of the money.

The Simplicity of Making Money has many high notes. These high notes are *The Simplicity of Making Money* as more and more money flow to one hand on the way to the bank.

Ending comment: make money baby make money!

And double those dollars. . .

Regularly, go to the bank!!!

Stop procrastinating!!!

And do it your way!!!

The Simplicity of Making Money

References

Clayton, N. (2011). Stay True to You: The definition of career success is up to you. *T+D, 65*(10), 8.

Shackle, E. (1999-2013). *Moolah, marigolds... and a macaroni!?!* Retrieved from Slang Euphemisms for 'Money': http://www.fun-with-words.com/money_words.html

Burka, J. B., & Yuen, L. M. (2008). *Procrastination : Why You Do It, What to Do About It Now*. Cambridge, MA: Da Capo/Life Long.

Krause, K., & Freund, A. M. (2013). How to Beat Procrastination: The Role of Goal Focus. *European Psychologist*, doi:10.1027/1016-9040/a000153

Stattler, E. (2013). The Value of Collaborating with Competitors. *Managing People At Work*, (370), 5.

Bartes, F. (2011). ACTION PLAN - BASIS OF COMPETITIVE INTELLIGENCE ACTIVITIES. *Economics & Management, 16*664-669.

Get Money Smarts. (n.d.). *Why Set Goals*. Retrieved from Get Money Smarts: http://www.getmoneysmarts.org/dream-smart/why-set-goals

Susan. (2010, January 9). *Top 10 Small Business Goals for the New Year*. Retrieved from New Earth Marketing : http://www.newearthmarketing.com/blogs/top-10-small-business-goals-new-year

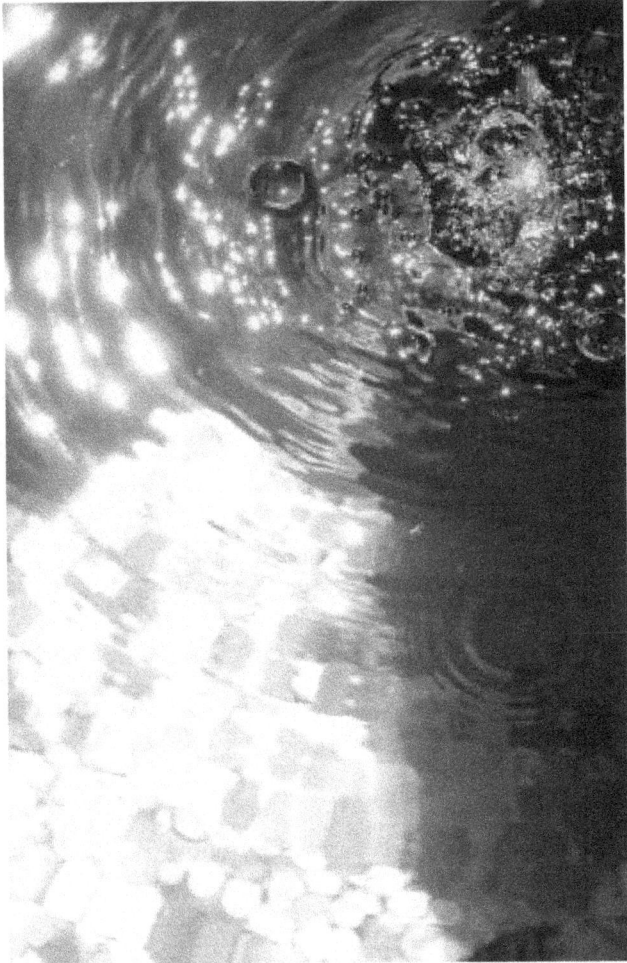

About the Author

Sherman A. Jones (Author) is currently working on his Masters Degree in Higher Education: Teaching on the Collegiate Level. Mr. Jones is currently president of Cbookspublishing and Bookstore.

The author, Sherman A. Jones has the following degrees:
➤ B. S. —Paralegal Studies
➤ B. S. —Theology
➤ A. S. —Radio and Television Broadcasting
➤ A. S. —Electronic Technology

The author, Sherman A. Jones, holds a lifetime FCC license.

www.ingramcontent.com/pod-product-compliance
Lightning Source LLC
Chambersburg PA
CBHW031614040426
42452CB00006B/521